crocodile

OR

alligator?

Susan Kralovansky

Consulting Editor, Diane Craig, M.A./Reading Specialist

Super Sandcastle

An Imprint of Abdo Publishing
www.abdopublishing.com

visit us at www.abdopublishing.com

Published by Abdo Publishing, a division of ABDO, PO Box 398166, Minneapolis, Minnesota 55439. Copyright © 2015 by Abdo Consulting Group, Inc. International copyrights reserved in all countries. No part of this book may be reproduced in any form without written permission from the publisher. Super SandCastle™ is a trademark and logo of Abdo Publishing.

Printed in the United States of America, North Mankato, Minnesota
062014
092014

Editor: Liz Salzmann
Content Developer: Nancy Tuminelly
Cover and Interior Design and Production: Mighty Media, Inc.
Photo Credits: Kelly Doudna, Shutterstock

Library of Congress Cataloging-in-Publication Data
Kralovansky, Susan Holt, author.
Crocodile or alligator? / Susan Kralovansky ; consulting editor, Diane Craig, M.A., reading specialist.
pages cm. -- (This or that?)
Audience: 004-010.
ISBN 978-1-62403-285-1
1. Crocodiles--Juvenile literature. 2. Alligators--Juvenile literature. I. Craig, Diane, editor. II. Title.
QL666.C925
597.98--dc23
2013041836

Super SandCastle™ books are created by a team of professional educators, reading specialists, and content developers around five essential components—phonemic awareness, phonics, vocabulary, text comprehension, and fluency—to assist young readers as they develop reading skills and strategies and increase their general knowledge. All books are written, reviewed, and leveled for guided reading, early reading intervention, and Accelerated Reader® programs for use in shared, guided, and independent reading and writing activities to support a balanced approach to literacy instruction.

contents

alligator or crocodile?

Is it an alligator? Or is it a crocodile? Can you tell the difference?

Alligators and crocodiles are both **reptiles**. The saltwater crocodile is the largest reptile on earth.

4

Alligators and crocodiles look a lot alike. They both have four short legs. They have strong tails. They have long **snouts**. And they have very sharp teeth!

u or v?

An alligator has a rounded **snout**. It is shaped like the letter U.

A crocodile has a pointed **snout**.
It is shaped like the letter V.

overbite or not?

Alligators have wide upper **jaws**. When their mouths are closed, you only see their top teeth. They have an overbite.

A crocodile's upper and lower **jaws** are the same size. This crocodile's mouth is closed. You can see its top and bottom teeth.

freshwater or saltwater?

Alligators live in **freshwater**. Lakes, streams, and **swamps** have freshwater.

Crocodiles can live in **saltwater** or **freshwater**.
Oceans and seas have salt water.

few or many?

There are two kinds of alligators. American alligators live in the southeastern United States. Chinese alligators live in a small area of China.

There are many kinds of crocodiles. They live in warm areas around the world.

nest or not?

A mother alligator builds a nest. She makes a mound of dirt and **twigs**. Then she lays eggs in the mound. She can lay up to 50 eggs.

Some **female** crocodiles build nests. Others dig holes in the sand. Some crocodiles lay up to 60 eggs.

powerful protectors

Most alligators and crocodiles guard their nests until the babies **hatch**.

Alligators and crocodiles also **protect** their babies until they can live by themselves.

at a glance

alligator ———————— crocodile

U-shaped **snout** ———————— V-shaped snout

upper **jaw** wider than lower jaw ———————— both jaws same size

lives in **freshwater** ———————— lives in freshwater or **saltwater**

two kinds ———————— many kinds

builds nest for eggs ———————— builds nest for eggs or digs hole

a gator tale craft

play along with this cool alligator puppet!

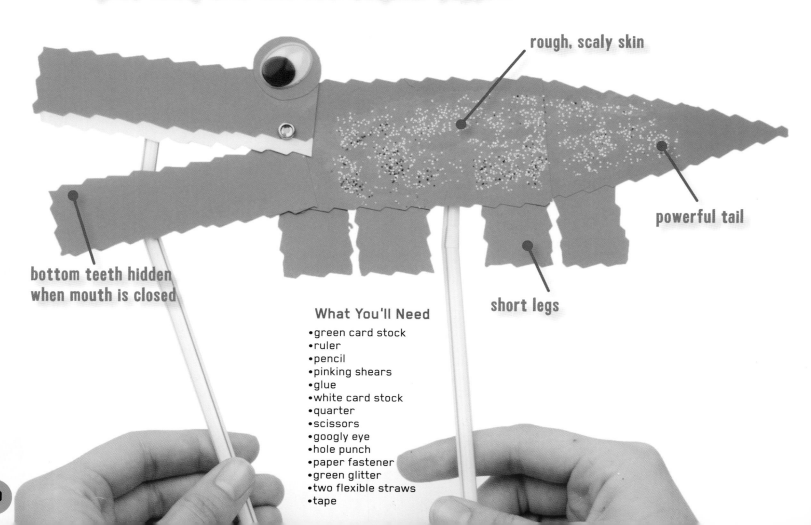

rough, scaly skin

powerful tail

short legs

bottom teeth hidden
when mouth is closed

What You'll Need
- green card stock
- ruler
- pencil
- pinking shears
- glue
- white card stock
- quarter
- scissors
- googly eye
- hole punch
- paper fastener
- green glitter
- two flexible straws
- tape

1. Draw four 4-inch (10 cm) by 2-inch (5 cm) rectangles on green card stock. Cut them out with pinking shears.

2. Cut one rectangle into a triangle. This is the tail. Choose another rectangle for the body. Glue the tail to a short side of the body. Cut the third rectangle into four equal pieces. These are the legs. Glue them to the body.

3. Cut the last rectangle in half **lengthwise**. Glue one half to the body just above the front legs. This is the lower **jaw**. The other half is the upper jaw.

4. Draw a 4-inch (10 cm) by 1-inch (2.5 cm) rectangle on white card stock. Cut it out with pinking shears. Glue them behind the upper jaw. They should stick out a little bit. Trace around the quarter on green card stock. Cut out the circle with regular scissors. Glue a googly eye to the circle. Glue the circle to the upper jaw.

5. Punch a hole in the upper jaw under the eye. Punch another hole in the front corner of the body. Put the upper jaw on top of the body so the holes line up. Put the paper fastener through the holes.

6. Put glue on the body and tail. Sprinkle green glitter over the glue. Let the glue dry. Turn the alligator over. Tape one straw to the upper jaw. Tape the other straw to the body. Move the alligator's mouth and body with the straws.

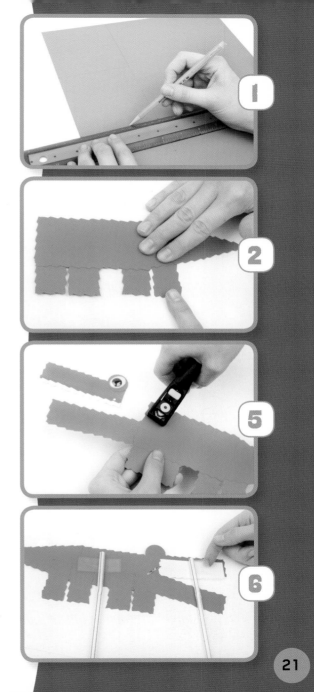

a croc tale craft

what's climbing out of the swamp? a crocodile puppet!

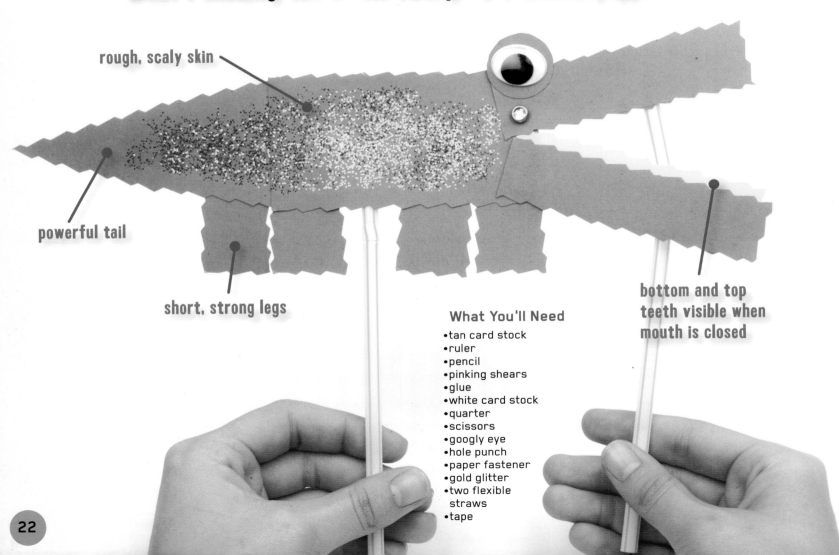

rough, scaly skin

powerful tail

short, strong legs

bottom and top teeth visible when mouth is closed

What You'll Need
- tan card stock
- ruler
- pencil
- pinking shears
- glue
- white card stock
- quarter
- scissors
- googly eye
- hole punch
- paper fastener
- gold glitter
- two flexible straws
- tape

1. Draw four 4-inch (10 cm) by 2-inch (5 cm) rectangles on tan card stock. Cut them out with pinking shears.

2. Cut one rectangle into a triangle. This is the tail. Choose another rectangle for the body. Glue the tail to a short side of the body. Cut the third rectangle into four equal pieces. These are the legs. Glue them to the body.

3. Cut the last rectangle in half **lengthwise** to make the **jaws**. Draw a 4-inch (10 cm) by 1-inch (2.5 cm) rectangle on white card stock. Cut it out with pinking shears. Glue them behind one of the jaw halves. They should stick out a little bit. This is the lower jaw. Glue it to the body just above the front legs.

4. Trace around the quarter on tan card stock. Cut out the circle with regular scissors. Glue a googly eye to the circle. Glue the circle to the upper jaw.

5. Punch a hole in the upper jaw under the eye. Punch another hole in the front corner of the body. Put the upper jaw on top of the body so the holes line up. Put the paper fastener through the holes.

6. Put glue on the body and tail. Sprinkle gold glitter over the glue. Let the glue dry. Turn the crocodile over. Tape one straw to the upper jaw. Tape the other straw to the body. Move the crocodile's mouth and body with the straws.

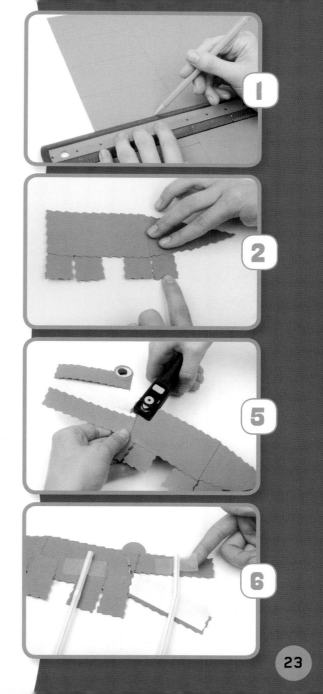

glossary

female – being of the sex that can produce eggs or give birth. Mothers are female.

freshwater – water that is not salty, such as a lake or river.

hatch – to break out of an egg.

jaw – one of the two bones in the face that teeth grow out of.

lengthwise – in the direction of the longest side.

protect – to guard someone or something from harm or danger.

reptile – a cold-blooded animal, such as a snake, turtle, or alligator, that moves on its belly or on very short legs.

saltwater – water that contains a lot of salt, such as an ocean.

snout – the jaws and nose of an animal.

swamp – an area of wet land often partly covered with water.

twig – a thin, small branch of a tree or a bush.